Ice Stylus

ALSO BY MARTIN ANDERSON

POETRY

The Kneeling Room *
The Ash Circle *
Heard Lanes
Dried Flowers
Swamp Fever
The Stillness of Gardens
Black Confetti
Belonging *
Snow. Selected Poems 1981–2011 *
Interlocutors of Paradise
The Lower Reaches *
Obsequy for Lost Things *

PROSE

The Hoplite Journals (complete in one volume) *

The Hoplite Journals I-XXIX *
The Hoplite Journals XXX-LIX *
The Hoplite Journals LX-LXXIX *

An asterisk denotes a Shearsman title.

Martin Anderson

Ice Stylus

Shearsman Books

First published in the United Kingdom in 2017 by
Shearsman Books
50 Westons Hill Drive
Emersons Green
BRISTOL
BS16 7DF

Shearsman Books Ltd Registered Office
30–31 St. James Place, Mangotsfield, Bristol BS16 9JB
(this address not for correspondence)

www.shearsman.com

ISBN 978-1-84861-520-5

Contents

"… how art thou come to this dark coast?"
Ezra Pound, *The Cantos*

Ground : Zero

"The vertical white weight that fell last night
And made their continent a blank."

David Gascoyne

Voyagers into silence, and into whiteness. Dissimulators. Inscribers of *blank* spaces. On the salt laden wind they listen for the cries of land birds. For surf pounding.

Names dissolved on the wind. "Roote[d] out from being." Inaudible breathings.

A land "free from blot or mixture." The whole of Europe dreaming. The same dream.

Unerwünscht. Over the empty spaces.

Peach and apple orchards, fields of corn. Burned, without pity. Storehouses full of squash, dried corn and beans. Houses with old men, women and children in them. "The stinck and sente … Frying in the frier." The ability to subsist depleted. Surviving on bark and roots. Hunger a knot of hard iron. "Let them eat grass."

A fluke of rusted iron in the heart. Poisons the tongue. Infects the hand that writes.

Scorn – on the white word. Shrivelled and parched. On the salt flat. Wintering in the throat. In "the land where no one weeps." In the eternal immiseration of snows.

Word: umbilicus. Nourished in earth. Our village. Our valley.
Seed shadow. The sound of its root-edness. Pleasing to us.

Those who fell, in a black ash swamp beside a river, far from home. They had the colour of freshly fallen snow on their hands and their feet.

Entire villages erased from the map. At evening, in the quietness of dusk, the Names.

"Black-earth country." The land sings. You could smell it on their breath. And when we left there were no more trails to follow.

Wading knee deep at times through snow. For months. Our bodies frozen. The sick and old stumbling after. The young in our arms and on our backs. In the dead of winter. Desiring food and shelter. Receiving only hard looks.

Snow

on upland embankments. On charred rafter and blackened stone of confiscated lands. Holding earth fast. On tidal creek. On reed-fringed wharf. The frozen weight of it. The silence.

The river's banks littered with ruined sacrariums, naves. The great walls gone: "very cumbrous to deface." Bodies taut under beams. All the swete musik torn down.

Cold, clear air. Beneath the levels the driftways empty. The river-dead rolled by the tide to the saltern's edges.

Small granite tower on a bluff. Blank interior. All its richly coloured illustrations of torment and suffering, demon and sinner, erased. Invisible under plasterer's daub, limer's brush. Under a thick layer of alabaster.

Echoing in chancel, in black thorn porch, the admonition "And the earth that is under thee shall be iron": the prayerful, unconfessed, drift of voices.

Snow

falling through such cold air. "Seized … driven off like wolves", the sacred fires in our lodges extinguished, "turning for one last look as [we] crossed the ridge". Later the skin on our feet would break. Flies lay eggs in our lacerations. On our breath our names would become barely recognizable.

The land. The land sings. But not, any longer, our songs. Our streams have all fallen silent.

Our most private parts, man woman and child, on the crowd thronged road back into the cheering town, draped over hat and pommel.

Ssippi. Our syllable water. Each letter a seed. Flowing through us. The land. Giving way to it. Touching, the tongue. Sound-shadow. Breath. Of a name. Askunessippi. All trace of it expunged from the map. To "cut off Remembrance of [us] from the Earth." Syllable. River. Syllable-shadow. "Hear me ... For I may never call again."

"Spring … every seed awakened … we yield to our neighbours, even our animal neighbours, the same right … to inhabit this land." *Ur-grund.* Ground: of all being. Of what *is*.

Tonight the ice clad spruce taps at the window as we move beneath it silent as ghosts. "The snow drift[ing] deep in the crooked gulch" remembers.

Ice Stylus

"Everything is real, and not real,
Both real and not real,
Neither real nor not real."

Nagarjuna

I

Here there are no true travellers, only wanderers through the lands, and the towns, of middle dimensions. Stemmers of the flow, launchers of those deluded "venture[s] against the unknown". Tamers of the nonexistent "wilderness".

Maps. The Thule – *Ultima* – of an imagination threatened. Engineers. Surveyors. Spies. Of a hideous vacuum. *Vacui*. Deep in the heart. "Love of possession was a disease with them."

Seeking riches – through that illusory "passage" – they ended up only avoiding themselves. "Motionless and menacing" (whose names were "like jewels in the night") stretching before them.

"Qallunaat"

        over the freezing floe. $11000 for a dry biscuit. Thinking they were navigating amidst things rather than re-presentations of them. What *manitou* under the auctioneer's gavel lingers?

We move, when we do move, only within our own space. Rapacious and restless. Crisscrossing the earth. Nomads. We can no longer be found on the quays of our unnecessary travels. Having taken to the air instead.

Silk handkerchiefs, a hair comb, scented soap, slippers and books. All that was left beneath the missing oarlocks. And a desperate note in a cairn. Somewhere far back in the frozen distance. A kettle of English flesh. The bones sang: "Don't give me anymore that rot about superior values…"

We carry this burning escriture in the palm of our hand. Ice stylus. Sea stylus. Uninhaleable air of our blind compass. Grazing the outer banks of where we begin and where we end.

Celebrity anchors. Big shot correspondents. With our Gucci medallions and our Armani suits. Mapping a way amidst apparitions, the fleeting phantoms of conjoined moments, assembling theodolites, in our hands the "great vanities, dreams and shadows of this vanishing life."

Exiles, we wake in the porticos of a foreign country. In our pockets nothing but the faded paper currency of our dreams – we have hawked our wares in the markets of an idle necessity. And when we look back we see that the way we came is simply the retracing of a worn out route.

"Fie. Fie." say the rollers breaking over our bows. "Do you not remember the frigate-bird on sun swept atolls its eyes burned out looking into the white plume, the blossoming white-hot cloud of darkness, of nothing? ... Do not forget the frigate-bird."

What we seize will, eventually, mock and forsake us. Each border we inscribe around ourselves will crumble. On the staircase there will be no one at the top to greet us. Only, descending, the taciturn remnant of a life that is walking from order into disorder without us.

We are an unmapped promontory, a frozen desolation. In the sea that keeps moving, white from an infinitude of patterns, there are no contending identities. Only precipices that vault. Fears assembled. Ice in our clothes, and in our boots.

To drive "away black care", regular streets and macadamed roads. ORDER. The essential attribute. The mind (city of god city of planning) divinely aloof from what it proposes.

Our "themed weekends" travel before us. From the car park tumulus of a dead king to the Blue Badge guide, to the aerial gondola. Aloft. Aloft. Set sail. Itineraries for scented isles. Strange incantations. Auguries of refulgence. Heading east into the self same seas where cartographers, once, drew islands that didn't exist. That explorers repeatedly reported sighting.

Adrift upon summer's indolent waters. Warm waters of an atoll. Upon an air of distressed contours. Will our boat crunch on the beach of that fierce light. Hand scribe the sign HC SVNT DRACONES (our own quietus a land so far it can't be seen). Turning everything that is dark into a devouring white?

Dust on those guano islands and their reefs. And on the exhausted seas about them. On that "City Beautiful. The White City" with "little brown men … who look like rats" and other exotic exhibits "blacker than buried midnight". Dust on the broken basilica knee deep in rubble. On the dowdy tear stained dais from which the actors still are leaving. Dust on the thousand irradiated quays and their goodbyes. On all the buntinged gangplanks rising after having performed their perfect obeisance to the shore.

II

Beyond all those habitations of middle dimensions, ghosts hover and congregate. Shadowy, in-substantial. On roads and against the walls of buildings, they appear and disappear. A pattern, a wave, moving in and out of the present. Unstable. Featureless. Unruly. Searching. Looking for us. On freezing rain swept streets we feel the cold draught of their passing.

From bankrupt, barely inhabitable cities, their piazzas empty, their administrative blocks darkening under acids of perpetual rain, from their broken skylights and the blocked drains of their lawless outskirts, we sing, under a canopy of leaves, a makeshift home of tarpaulin and sticks, the sound of an emancipated longing in our ears, of unfurbished days and nights.

To own the air around us. A thing so designated: unseen, unheard, untouched. Licit domicilium. Not apportioned, measured or weighed. No lighter, heavier than our desires. Continually making and remaking us. Who'll issue a patent for it? Who'll turn it into shares?

After all our wanderings, sun-baked, salt-scoured, ice-scarred, over inhospitable continents and seas, we returned. To a dubious homespun ontology. To *peiras*, a demarking etched into the world too deep to be erased. To a *Fata Morgana* moving, always, within us. Leaving no stretch of land or sea uncharted. That shifting uncalcined and untrammelled space within us – banished.

Our fathers fought in the desert, for an obsolete empire. Year after year, chasing the shadow of an elusive enemy. His campfires and his middens buried. Each day the wind shifted the terrain so that the way forward became the way by which they had arrived. Puzzled. Dazzled by sun glare. Beset by mirages. Their maps useless. They wandered for years amid plundered mosaics and the ruined temples of former empires. Watching the stars. Listening in the night wind to the approach of imaginary armies.

And nightly here we sit our head in the dark alcove, listening. To a name that is intrinsically restless, inherently absent. To a dark energy unadorned by substance. And in the silence we curate our collection of perdurable objects, our glass cabinet frantically rattling as an open door lets in the wind.

What false Arcadia at the sill still beckons? We were warned but we went on, with our empty pilgrimages, our spoiled wine, to the glacier's foot. Having chosen, all along, the wrong route. Our oarlocks rusted. Our rudder half sheared off. Unaware each destination alters with each new trajectory from which it is approached.

And Alexander (that footloose traveller) of Macedon's illustrious tutor had, amongst many, one curious shortcoming. He conducted himself "as if he were analysing things and not ideas."

Each river that we forded subverted. Each successive surge and seethe, each roil of each letter as it slithered and torqued morning and evening over the tongue. That *same* river, which "did not change its position nor remain at rest", was neither present nor absent.

Under the oar's heave the pull and pluck of longing. That vast and dim interior in which the mind magnifies itself, and is extinguished. Unwrought silence of the descending. There is no end to it. And no beginning.

Torn up map, edge of a sea that can't be crossed, desk and lamp. The upright shadow of a man plotting a course between shadows and phantasms. Voices of friends and comrades rise and fall with the wind. They are unable to hear themselves, and the man at the desk reciting their names, from so deep within the sea's disorder.

At the gate and at the window, the ideal outline of an ideal object. Conflations of sense perceptions. Episodes of mind. Point us toward an empty room. A bare space where there are no formations.

Looking into that white plume, that blossoming white-hot cloud of darkness, of nothing.

Unsubdued Singing

"The Absolute has no history"

F.H. Bradley

I

In a dead place where there was no echo. No houses. The wind rolled on without obstruction. The only sound was the wind. The calloused tread of the foot going where it had been already. The roadside shrines, indicating those who would not return. Beneath the stands of jujube and carob. A mist before their eyes. Calling out to the ghosts of their former selves. To those who would come after.

They left no footprints in the sand when they were leaving. Light footed as ghosts they drifted with their possessions over the dark waterways and sluices. Saying not a word to each other. Into the fading light they departed.

The land they laid bare they left behind them. Scorched rock. Embers. Corpses along the wayside and in the orchards. Contaminated water. What was the land to them? And the people? A staging ground, merely, for their adventures.

II

The past a buried mausoleum. A broken catenation. What shadow upon their precarious present rested. What fragment rehearsing its own death. Tolled like a buoy on the irremediable current. On air too thin to support its own weight? It sank back, whilst surging forward, destined to forget. Leaf shadow on a step. A sunlit capstan. Creak of pleated rope fibre across a bow, its swirling motes. Who, in that light of fragments, did not remember the Mechanic's lament: "History is more or less bunk ... We don't need [it]."

A delirium of spent images. Placing the eucharist of what they consumed, and what consumed them, on the tongue. A word, a thing. There was no difference. A liturgy of empty sound: "What is bought and traded *is* (on, now, dead man's dump) consecrated again and again by what is New".

Unsure whether they had landed, or were just setting off. Watching the shore line. The water a ceaseless movement, backward and forward. Erasing all trace of where they were. No point of reference. No stable coordinates. Except the land. That phantasmal inheritance of a mind sore-pressed – to come into possession of its own self. Rubbing the little stone idol at the mast head. Delivering prayers in the fo'c'sle. To imbue with shape all that flotsam of drifting sense. To restrain the incubus. Enshrine an order.

Past white capped rocks on furious isthmuses they proceeded. The wind in their ears. Oblivious to silence. In the shearwater's bill a creature of the deep. A momentary shadow against the topsail. Before it was released back into darkness. Ropes thrumming in wind. Hair blown back. In the strain of timbers forward. An unconscionable laugh. The hauteur of unattainable horizons.

To have seized, in that delirium, the path to an unexplored evening heavy with the scent of pine, where the air held a long looked for confirmation of why they set out. Sure footed amid the snares of history. Clearing their way over revetments and roads of bone. Appropriators of a gaze, *Oculus Mundi*, fixed steadily upon the stars. Upon all their awkward alignments and conjunctions.

Between one sandy entrepot and another wind blew. Stones of ancient highways lay scattered at their edges. The names rose and fell. Dromedary days lingered. Under an amputated sky blast walls absorbed the rush of air. The present endlessly inscribed within itself. Fossilized dung amid the ruins. Shards from shaping hands that had vanished.

Mapmakers. Of Elsewhere. Guiding the hand and mind through recalcitrant waters. Soteriological cargoes. Incense of engorged holds. Within that ideal order to which the present adverts. Interdicting the return.

To stand in the fragrant pharmacopoeia of the future. Breathing a pure air. All epaulets ("nailed into naked shoulders") and instantiations. Dust on their collars. The exhausted sediment of their travels. At the bottom of the pond the dark gnomon dissolved. Paradisial vapours rising and dispersing, filling their mouths.

III

Dissolved moment. Unnavigable sensum. And on the long road that stretches from it an eternity of longing. An unexculpated journey. Hymn to the not moving. How History ignores the moment. Compiling, instead, its aggregate of false clues. Its granary of composited diversions. Who, in fact, writes the history in which one believes one is living?

Broken amulets and broaches. Artefacts of a different order. Carbonised bone, hair and flesh. The trowel of a blunt archaeology, unearthing nothing. Except, in those two fiercely irradiated cities, penumbras that might have been persons. Rather than 'savages', spent images for discarding.

Heading into death lands. The dark cold points of a far north that is always calling. Beneath the bright summer foliage. The hand moving the curtain. Implicate, always, in each border one constructs round object and act. Ordering, day in day out, the afternoon and the evening that will succeed one.

IV

There, where there was no longer any current, any sea swell or wash of wave against them, they beheld, on the sand white littoral where the air with its fragrant exhalation had encalmed them, an unfamiliar spirit or apparition, walking out of the trees down to the water, a sprig of pine in its hand, beckoning to them to follow.

Sylvanus. In the deep wood: "salvages". "Veraye brute". A crying. A panick. Through pine groves, "extreame thicke". "God give to us the order, and the serenity, of a Garden".

Overgrown. In shadow. The mind is. To such a degree they could penetrate no further. Hugging the coast line. Fording the estuaries. The sound of birds all around them. An unsubdued singing. So tame they would have eaten out of their hands if they had food for them.

Scent of pine on the air. Sudorific. Of another order. Over everything yellow sulphurous waft of pollen. Ripple of night wind across a river. Be-*wildered*. Without a path. To lose their way in "a wilderness" of unfamiliar signs and voices. Following the artifice of compass, ruler. Into time's lost thickets and days. Into a different time, of day, of year. Of place. Unaware they were in it. That they had left that absolute order of their own.

Where swamp maple and dogwood are in bloom. Their petals adrift on abraded water. Dark, oleaginous green under banks. White, over the granite bed, scintillant at the centre. Incessant, migratory movement. Leaving no record of where it began. Or will end.

"'I give to you a red road' … All [things] walking on the good red road together."

Over the bloodstained roads the voice of time. Beating the backwoods, searching the underbrush, the tangled roots round crumbling columns, for it. "Tempus Fugit". In the light of a day that is swiftly running away from itself. Into the cracked basin of the fountain on the lawn. Only to enter again, beyond the window overlooking them, the woods that are empty of it.

Notes

Ground : Zero

Terms for toponomy and hydronomy are the most durable designations within landscape and form the most stable substratum of linguistic evidence for the identity of human habitation. Numerous indigenous river names in North America, however, were sacrificed to that of the River Thames (page 23) in England. In England its name, significantly, survived the depredations of Roman, Saxon, Dane and Norman (and perhaps even Celt).

Sketch

Detail, from an informant's sketch, of Chief Elkhair's depiction during the Delaware Indian Big House Ceremony of the human life-spirit's journey after death. "Attendants use the wing feathers of noble, 'pure' birds, helpers of man ... with which the Path to his final destiny is brushed clean". As his spirit approaches "where roads cross" it is led, if he has followed a righteous path, up a high mountain where it meets the huge thunder bird, the "storm maker". Beyond this point lies the Abode of thunder and tempests. And beyond these terrifying heights is a still more distant ridge of mountains. The final stage of the journey, glimpsed still further off, lies within the Abode of Getantowit, the Great Spirit. [From *A Study of the Delaware Indian Big House Ceremony V2* by Frank G. Speck, Pennsylvania Historical Commission, 1931.]

www.ingramcontent.com/pod-product-compliance
Lightning Source LLC
Chambersburg PA
CBHW020213090426
42734CB00008B/1051